Copyright © 2025 Exaltation Press

Author: Tatiana Korshunova
Illustrator: Valeria Nerucheva
Translator: Fr. John Hogg
Editor: Sally Boyle

"The Life of the Holy New-martyr Eli"
This book is part of the series Lives of Saints for Children. In this story, children will learn about the life of St. Elizabeth the New-Martyr, a woman of great humility, courage, and love who remained faithful to Christ even in the face of suffering and sacrifice.

All rights reserved. This book or any portion thereof may not be reproduced or used in any manner whatsoever without the express written permission of the publisher except for the use of brief quotations in a book review.

Translated from the original "Житие святой Елизаветы Новомученицы в пересказе для детей" by Nikea Press, Copyright © Trading House «NIKEA», www.Nikeabooks.ru

ISBN: 978-1-950067-93-0 (Hardcover)
       978-1-950067-94-7 (Paperback)

First printing edition 2025

Exaltation Press
Grand Rapids, MI

www.ExaltationPress.com

For bulk orders, please contact editor@exaltationpress.com

Help us build our permanent temple for future generations! Scan this QR-code to donate to Holy Cross Antiochian Orthodox Church in Grand Rapids, MI. Thank you and God bless you!

Tatiana Korshunova

The Life of St. Elizabeth the New-Martyr

Retold for Children

Illustrations by

Valeria Nerucheva

Grand Rapids · Exaltation Press · 2024

What is humility? It is meekness and obedience – and one of the most essential Christian virtues. The monks who live in desert monasteries obtain humility through complete obedience to their teachers, their "spiritual fathers." For example, an elder might say, "Put this stick in the ground and water it." His disciple doesn't argue; he just waters it. Because of the disciple's obedience and humility, sometimes a miracle happens, and the old dry stick is covered with young leaves.

Monks and nuns spend their entire lives striving to gain humility through obedience and meekness. But is it possible to be humble while living in a palace, wearing fine clothing and jewelry, eating off of plates of gold and silver, and riding in a fine carriage? Yes, it turns out that it is possible. You don't have to go to the desert to find this virtue – as long as you give yourself in obedience to God and dedicate your life to doing good for others.

Elizabeth – the granddaughter and great-granddaughter of kings, and the wife of an emperor's son – dedicated her whole life to her neighbor. She began with her own family: lovingly obeying her parents, and when her mother died, becoming like a mother to her younger sisters and brother. Then, when she was married, she listened to her beloved husband about everything. Later on, she became a great mother to all of Moscow.

Everything started out like a fairy tale. In a German duchy (called Hesse-Darmstadt) there was a princess named Elizabeth—a precious little girl called Ella, who had blue eyes, golden hair, and chubby little cheeks. She had an older sister, two younger sisters, and a brother. Their mom and dad loved them very much. Since they loved them so much, do you think their parents gave them sweets and ice cream on a golden tray for breakfast? Did they let them play all day with horses while drinking lemonade? No, their food was very simple, and they weren't allowed to be lazy. They were raised to be noble, which meant learning not to think about themselves, always remembering their duty before God, working hard, and telling the truth.

The prince and princesses spent a lot of time studying and learning music and sports. They, of course, knew English and

German because their father was a German duke and their mother was the daughter of the Queen of England. They struggled with French, however. (Ella wasn't the best student, and even as an adult, she made mistakes when writing in French.) Their castle had an enormous library, with paintings by famous artists and collections of antiques, minerals, shells, and fossils. The whole family loved to read, draw, and observe nature.

Although they had plenty of servants, the girls cleaned their own rooms, made their own beds, and lit the fire in the fireplace. The girls were taught how to run a household. They learned to do everything around the house, and that helped them later in life. One of the things the Christian faith teaches is that it's good to try to be self-sufficient, rather than always relying on others.

Their mother, a princess, spent a lot

of money helping the poor, and every day she visited hospitals, orphanages, and homes for the infirm, taking her children with her. How many of us find it difficult to visit our own grandmothers in the hospital! But every Saturday, the princesses of Hesse-Darmstadt brought flowers to the hospital to give to patients they usually didn't even know.

Ella had a friend named Sergei, a boy who was seven years older than she was. They often

played together in a neighboring castle where his mother, the Russian empress, was staying for a long visit. Her younger sons, the Grand Dukes Sergei and Paul ("Grand Duke" was the title given to male members of the imperial family), played with the princesses of Hesse-Darmstadt. Sergei would often stop playing with the others to spend time with young Ella instead. He would gently take her by the arm, and they would walk together along the park trails.

As soon as Ella grew up, Sergei asked her to marry him, and she agreed. Grand Duke Sergei Alexandrovich, with his gray eyes and tall, slim frame, and the lovely princess Elizabeth walked around Darmstadt, happy and cheerful. They were both shy, and if you didn't know them well, you might think that they were haughty or boring. In reality, though, they both loved to laugh and joke around. Ella's fiancé immediately started teaching her to speak and write in Russian, which brought them many pleasant and cheerful moments together.

The princess, along with her father and sisters, went to Russia at Pentecost. It was the beginning of summer, with flowers blooming all around, and Sergei had their train decorated

with white flowers. At every station, the flower wreaths were replaced, and the scent of lilies of the valley, jasmine, and lilacs made the northern landscape especially delightful.

At Peterhof, Sergei introduced his bride-to-be to his brother, the tsar, and the whole Romanov royal family. They were all delighted with the princess. TThe groom's cousin, the great poet Constantine Romanov, wrote in his diary, "She walked modestly and shyly, like a vision, like a dream." (At that time, modesty and shyness were thought to make a young woman more beautiful.) Throughout her life, Princess Elizabeth would blush when she got excited, which only made her more beautiful!

Elizabeth did have good reason to feel timid. Russia, with its large open spaces, was nothing like the cozy little German principalities. The Neva River was wider than any river in Germany, and the vast public squares, grand avenues of St. Petersburg, and the marble halls of the Winter Palace – with miles of glistening wooden floors – were unlike anything she had ever seen before. On

top of all that, the Russian princesses were surrounded by crowds of ladies-in-waiting and courtiers, while government officials and servants were always bustling about.

After their wedding, Sergei and Ella went to his Ilinskoe estate, outside of Moscow, for their honeymoon. Ella immediately felt right at home in the noble manor and began to look after her subjects. She went from cottage

to cottage to see how the peasants were living, and she was horrified! There she found poverty, filth, and not a single hospital. She immediately asked her husband to send for a good midwife from the city to help the peasant women give birth to healthy children. Sergei Alexandrovich, who adored his wife, quickly did what she asked and then built a maternity home in the village as well. Grand Duchess Elizabeth became so well-regarded among the peasants that, when the children born there were baptized, she was often chosen as their godmother.

In Ilinskoe, they lived a quiet family life, without all the ceremony and formality of palace life. TThe grand duchess was living by the advice she herself gave at nineteen: store up health and happiness while you're young, so that later, you'll have the strength you need.

How the peasants loved her! At charity lotteries and bazaars, everyone wanted her to be the one to hand them their prizes or purchases. One elderly peasant came from over seventy-five miles away just to admire her.

"Point her out to me," he asked. "I've heard a lot about her, and I want to see what she's like, whether she's really as kind and really loves the people as much as people say." At first, he couldn't figure out where she was, since he thought he was looking for some majestic lady in a crown. Finally, she came up to him and smiled her angelic smile.

He looked at her for a long time, crossed himself, and said, "Glory to God that I was counted worthy to see you, my little princess!"

She bowed to him and asked respectfully, "What would you like to buy, Grandfather?"

"Mother," he said, answering her

respectfully, "I can't buy anything. Give me something. I don't have any money."

She looked around the table at the bazaar and picked out a nice teacup, saucer, and spoon.

"Grandfather, do you want this cup? Do you like it?"

"I like it very much, my little princess."

She told them to wrap the gift.

"Goodbye, Grandfather," she said sweetly, trying delicately to slip a ten-ruble note into his hand. But he didn't notice the money and thought she was just shaking his hand. He grabbed her hand and kissed it a few times, the way that people kiss icons. The grand duchess then noticed that the money had fallen on the ground and pointed it out to him.

"I wonder who dropped that!" he said in surprise.

"That's your money, Grandfather. I gave it

to you to take with you on the road."

At first, he didn't want to take it, but Duchess Elizabeth said, "No, grandfather, take it. Good-bye! I have to go now. Others are waiting for me."

He stood by the counter at the bazaar, unable to walk away, just watching her.

"They were right to praise her. What a beauty! When she smiles, she looks like one of the angels they paint in the icons. I'll never forget the way she welcomed me. I'll tell everyone when I get home."

There were many such stories. Grand Duchess Elizabeth joined the Orthodox Church in 1891, on Lazarus Saturday, and was given the middle name Fyodorovna – traditionally given to German princesses who became Orthodox – in honor of the Feodorovskaya Icon of the Mother of God, which was especially revered by the

royal family. On Pascha, for the first time, she took communion with her husband, and the last barrier between them disappeared. They lived as happily as only those who are close to each other spiritually and dedicated to each other can.

Only one thing saddened them. Years passed, but no children were born. The grand duke was a strict man who could be stern with his nieces and nephews; he didn't tolerate troublemakers and would scold them appropriately for every misdeed. On the other hand, he would go swimming with them, put the little ones to bed, and give them goodnight kisses—all of which the parents of these noble children never did.

One of the little princesses once said that she trusted Uncle Sergei completely, even when they were in a boat, sailing on a summer lake, heading towards a waterfall.

He sat near her and, holding her tightly, said in a soft, calming voice, "Don't be afraid, darling. Even if the boat capsizes, we won't drown. I know how to swim."

Children simply fell in love with Elizabeth because she was so kind and as pretty as a fairy tale princess. Seeing her for the first time, one little boy who was a count didn't even notice when the empress started to talk to him.

"Look at me!" she said, smiling as she gently took his chin and turned his head toward her. Then she gave him a kiss and asked him where he had been looking.

"I was looking at Grand Duchess Elizabeth, Your Majesty."

The empress laughed and said, "Now I understand. I'll let her know."

What a happy time it was in Ilinskoe, when Sergei's favorite younger brother, Paul, married a Greek princess named Alexandra and she gave birth to a daughter, Maria! The brothers' wives, Elizabeth and Alexandra, became very good friends and even sewed identical dresses. All too soon, however, young Alexandra died after going into premature labor with her second child. The premature baby boy survived, thanks to the care of his aunt and uncle, but his father was so sick with grief that he left the country to try to recover.

Grand Duke Sergei and Grand Duchess Elizabeth, then, became the adoptive parents to Maria, who was a year and a half old, and little baby Dmitri. They gave them baths, swaddled them, looked after them, and played with them. They raised and taught them and took them to Church.

"Of course, I couldn't love my own children any more than I love yours," Sergei wrote to his brother who was far away.

In 1891, the tsar made Grand Duke Sergei the governor-general of Moscow, which was a very important position. Even though Moscow wasn't the capital city at that time, it had always been the chief Russian city, and governing it wasn't an easy task. As the wife of the governor-general of Moscow, the grand duchess also had a lot of work to do in helping to care for the poor of Moscow. There were wealthy people who wanted to give money to the poor or help them in some other way, but everything needed to be arranged and organized. Someone had to carefully track how much was donated and how much was distributed. It was very serious work, but Elizabeth handled it wonderfully. Soon people were competing with each other to get her to be the chairwoman of various charitable organizations and the patroness of various God-pleasing institutions.

In 1904, Russia went to war with Japan. In the Kremlin Palace, the grand duchess organized a whole army of women – from the simplest to the richest and noblest – who worked together from morning until evening, gathering and sending packages with medicine, bandages, food, warm clothing, icons, and books to the front.

Every day, Elizabeth Fyodorovna, wearing a simple gray or light blue dress, would go around to the workshops where these packages were put together. No matter what mistakes or slip-ups her inexperienced coworkers made, she never lost patience with them and would gladly do any difficult task herself.

On February 4, 1905, while she was on her way to visit the workshops, she heard a horrible explosion nearby. All the windowpanes of the palace shattered. Grand Duchess Elizabeth stood for a moment with her hand pressed to her heart, realizing that the terrible event she and her husband had long feared had finally come to pass.

In the past few years, Sergei had often said that the revolutionaries hated him and were getting ready to make an attempt on his life. Just as he feared, he had now been killed in a bomb explosion and had died at the hands of terrorists! (Later on, in 1917, when the revolutionaries overthrew the tsar and took over the government, these same revolutionaries wiped out hundreds of thousands, even millions of the best people of Russia.)

When the grand duchess came home, heartbroken and exhausted, she put on a black dress of mourning and sat down to write telegrams to their relatives. How on earth would she be able to tell them the awful news? With what could she comfort them? She knew, however, that she had to try, because she

always wanted to help others. "The Lord has taken our dear Sergei. He didn't suffer. Let us pray together, and God will give us strength," she wrote to Sergei's brother Paul.

She was then informed that her husband's driver was seriously injured in the explosion and would soon die. Elizabeth took off her mourning dress, put on the light blue dress she usually wore, and went to the hospital. The faithful servant, whispering with difficulty, asked her how the grand duke was and whether he was alive. Elizabeth gave him a kind smile and said, "He sent me to you." Comforted by her words, the driver soon passed away. He was buried before Sergei Alexandrovich, and the grand duchess followed the driver's casket the entire way, stayed for the funeral, and even went to the cemetery outside Moscow for the burial.

Elizabeth's composure, meekness,

and submission to the will of God amazed everyone. She didn't think about herself, only about others. She received visitors who came to express their sympathy, answered a multitude of telegrams and letters, and tried, as much as she was able, to comfort and calm those who were weeping along with her.

On the second or third day after her husband's death, Elizabeth secretly went to the prison to visit Kalyayev, the revolutionary who had murdered her husband—to forgive him! She hoped that he would repent and that his unhappy soul would open up to her.

Elizabeth went into the room alone. Kalyayev was so surprised that, at first, he didn't recognize her.

"Who are you?" he asked.

"I am the grand duke's widow."

"I didn't want to kill you! A few times I had the bomb ready, but you were with

him. So I didn't...."

"How could you not realize that when you killed him you were killing me as well? But I forgive you, both for myself and for him. Only repent, I beg you! Look, I brought you a copy of the Gospels. Read it and I will be praying to God to forgive you."

"I will not repent, and I'm not sorry for what I did!" the murderer answered.

Nevertheless, Elizabeth left the Gospel book and a small icon in the room. Who knows? Maybe through her prayers this criminal was able to remember God in his final moments. By doing this, the grand duchess imitated Christ who, from the Cross, forgave those who had crucified Him. She even had the Savior's words, "Father, forgive them, for they know not what they do," carved on a memorial cross that was put on the roadside where the murder had taken place.

After her husband's death, Elizabeth Fyodorovna stopped going out into society entirely. Most likely, she would have followed the example of the early saints by selling all she had and going into the desert to live in a monastery. However, her adopted children who had just lost their dear uncle still hadn't grown up, and so she kept living the way that she always had—for other people. This way of living is one of the most direct paths to holiness. It may sound simple, but living for other people instills in us the humility through which we ascend on high.

Four years passed. The children were grown. Grand Duchess Maria Pavlovna married a Swedish prince, and Grand Duke Dmitri applied to an officer cavalry school and moved to St. Petersburg.

It was at that time that Elizabeth gave away and sold all her valuable possessions and bought a manor on Bolshaya Ordynka Street by the Moscow River. There she had the Martha and Mary Convent of Mercy constructed—a convent and home for sisters of mercy living under the guidance of a priest. They prayed, cared for the sick, raised orphans, and visited the poor, doing all of this lovingly, with care and affection. Elizabeth believed that this would turn hearts to Christ and bring the light of Christ to the unfortunate. There were so many people who wanted to join the convent! This was because many young women wanted to serve God alongside Grand Duchess

Elizabeth.

The buildings of the convent were designed by a wonderful architect, and the iconography in the churches was done by a talented artist. (Thank God, the Soviet authorities didn't destroy the convent, and today, you can go to Bolshaya Ordynka Street and walk around the gardens and pray in the Church of the Protection of the Theotokos, where everything is just like it was in Elizabeth's time. In the abbess's rooms, there are now new wicker chairs "in an antique style," but the piano is the very same one that she used to play.)

When she moved to the convent, the grand duchess left the palace for three modest rooms, where she slept on a wooden bed with no mattress and a hard pillow, and even then, barely slept three hours a day. She studied medicine and worked in the convent just like the other sisters, only with more duties since, as the abbess, she had to be involved in everything. For example, on one occasion in the winter, someone needed to sort through vegetables in the basement. The sisters started arguing because none of them wanted to have to deal with dirty, rotten potatoes. Mother Elizabeth didn't say anything; she just got dressed in her work clothes and went to do it herself. Only then did the others hurry to help her.

Elizabeth fasted all year round. On great feasts, when bishops would gather together in the convent, she would put a piece of fish on her plate, but it would stay there, untouched. At midnight, she got up to pray and then went to do her rounds at the hospital. If one of the patients was in bad shape, she would stay and take care of him until the morning.

The medical care in the convent hospital

was so good that other hospitals in the city sent their most severe patients there. Once, a cook accidentally knocked a kerosene stove over on herself and was burned so badly that, even today, saving her would have been difficult. But Mother Elizabeth took it upon herself to change the woman's bandages and spent two and a half hours each morning and evening with her, pausing throughout the painful bandaging process to calm and comfort her. To the doctors' surprise, the woman recovered.

Well-known surgeons often asked Elizabeth to assist during difficult operations because she never lost her calm or composure and promptly did as they requested. Many people were amazed at how she was able to overcome her disgust at the sight of blood and horrible injuries and how she was able to put up with the strong putrid smells of the hospital, even though she was such a noble woman who loved the smell of wild flowers. Her life at the convent and hospital was a good illustration to us of how any ascetic labors are accomplished. To accomplish any good work, you often have to make yourself do it, to force yourself to take the first step. There's even a saying: "Only the first step is difficult." After that, the rest becomes easier, as long as you keep repeating to yourself, "Lord, have mercy."

Elizabeth was a true woman of prayer. She constantly prayed quietly under her breath, and in church she stood there straight and still, like a candle. There were even many times when people saw her crying during the services. With her blessing, an underground chapel had been built below the main church altar, and it was dedicated to the Heavenly Powers. During Divine Liturgy, she would go down there to pray without being seen. Even though she was strict with herself, as the mother abbess she was neither stern, nor gloomy, nor closed-off, because true Christians really do rejoice without ceasing, as God has commanded. Just like in her childhood and throughout her marriage, she was able to laugh and joke.

Once when her older sister, Princess Victoria, was visiting the convent, Victoria's door opened just a little bit early in the morning, and someone with a shaved head peeked in and said hello. The princess was scared at first, thinking that some naughty child had made his way into the monastery. Then she realized that it was just her own sister Ella, without her monastic veil and with her hair cut short, peeking in to surprise her.

"We lived like we were in paradise," one of the sisters of the convent later recalled. Mother Elizabeth was like a mother to them, and she loved them like they were her own children. And how much good they were able to accomplish!

The year 1917 arrived, and the revolutionaries finally got what they wanted. The tsar abdicated the throne, and six months later, the Bolsheviks – who did not believe in God and violently persecuted all who did – came to power. Since Elizabeth was a German princess, she was given the chance to leave the country. A Swedish envoy came to Moscow on behalf of the German emperor specifically to convince her to leave Russia. The grand duchess missed her relatives in Darmstadt very much, but she answered firmly: "I can't leave the convent, my patients, and the sisters that God has entrusted into my care. I'm staying here."

On another occasion, a simple cobbler, whose wife was being cared for in the convent, offered to come get Elizabeth in his sleigh and take her to a safe place. She thanked him and said with a smile, "The sisters won't all fit in your sleigh."

In the spring of 1918, on the third day after Pascha when the Iviron icon of the Theotokos is celebrated, a car full of Red Army officers came to get Elizabeth. She asked them to give her two hours so that she could go around the convent and give instructions to the sisters. They refused and only gave her a half an hour. Everyone, including the priest, was

praying in the hospital church on their knees, but when the army officers took Elizabeth, the sisters rushed towards her, holding onto her and saying, "We won't let you take our mother!" They cried and yelled, but the army officers pushed them away with the butts of their rifles and took Elizabeth, her cell attendant Barbara, and one of the sisters named Katherine. As they drove away, the priest stood on the steps of the church, crying and blessing them over and over again.

The grand duchess and her companions were then put on a train bound for the Urals. She wrote two letters to the convent from the road.

"We're doing very well. There's snow everywhere. I can't forget yesterday, all of your dear, kind faces. O Lord, what suffering there was in them; my heart was sick. Always be not only my children but also obedient pupils. Pull together and be like one soul, all of it for God, and say like St. John Chrysostom, 'Glory to God for all things.'"

"My dear children, glory to God that you all took communion. You all stood before the Savior as if you were one soul. You remember that I was often afraid that you all found your strength for life in my support, and I told you: 'You need to cling more closely to God!' The Lord says, 'My son, give me your heart and may your eyes observe my paths.' Then be sure that if you give Him your heart, that is yourself, you are giving God everything. Right now, we are all living through the same thing, and against our will we find comfort only in Him to carry our cross of being parted from each other. The Lord has decided that it is time for us to carry His cross. Let us try to be worthy of this joy."

Elizabeth and the other two sisters were taken to Alapaevsk in the Perm region and put

in a school on the edge of the town. Members of the Romanov royal family were also brought there—Grand Dukes Sergei Mikhailovich, the brothers John, Constantine, and Igor, and Prince Vladimir Paley, along with their servants. The prisoners were allowed some freedom. They went to church and took walks in the field near the school. They cleaned the schoolyard themselves and arranged the flower beds and vegetable gardens.

Elizabeth, an experienced gardener, took charge of planting the vegetables. In her room, she prayed a lot and drew. In the evenings, they all gathered together to read their evening prayers before bed.

Having been sent into exile, they all knew why they had been brought to this God-forsaken place—even if you tried to run away, there would be nowhere to run to. After they had spent more than six months in this captivity and exile, Lenin decided to destroy not only the overthrown tsar, Nicholas, his wife, Alexandra, and their children (who were being held in a similar way in Ekaterinburg) but also all the other members of the Romanov family. Elizabeth and Sister Barbara, who stayed with her voluntarily, started preparing themselves for death and prayed to God to strengthen them.

A local girl who brought groceries to the prisoners later recounted, "Mother Elizabeth would come out on the porch and take the basket with tears on her face. She'd turn around, wipe away the tears, and say, 'Thank you, dear girl, thank you!' When I was with them for the last time, she came out, took the basket, and told me to wait. She returned a few minutes later and gave me back the basket (like she always did), but it had something in it. 'We don't have long to live. Remember us,' she said,

with tears in her eyes. I ran home with the basket, and there in it was some pink fabric to make a dress."

On July 17, 1918, in Ekaterinburg, the royal family was shot. After midnight that night, on July 18, the feast of St. Sergius of Radonezh (who was especially loved by Elizabeth), the prisoners in Alapaevsk were led into a forest and thrown into an abandoned, submerged mineshaft. Grenades were then thrown in after them.

Several months after they were killed, Alapaevsk was taken by the White Army, an army that included many Christians and was fighting against the Bolsheviks. The martyrs' bodies were removed from the mineshaft, and their caskets were placed in a cemetery church where priests served funeral services for them. However, the Red Army soon retook the area, and Igumen Seraphim (Kuznetsov) from Perm managed, with great difficulty, to take the eight coffins to the city of Chita and from there to China. They didn't arrive in Beijing until April 1920.

Elizabeth's sisters and brother later requested that her body and that of Sister Barbara be sent to Jerusalem and buried in the Russian Orthodox Church of St. Mary Magdalene on the Mount of Olives. Now, pilgrims from all over the world come to the Russian church in Jerusalem to pray at the grave of St. Elizabeth—for the health of their loved ones, to ask for help in doing works of charity, and for help in all good works that are pleasing to God, who is glorified in His saints.

www.ingramcontent.com/pod-product-compliance
Lightning Source LLC
Chambersburg PA
CBHW052126070526
44586CB00016B/2097